Becoming Like Your Teacher

Developing Effective Church Planting Apprenticeships

. . . .

Rev. Bob Engel
Rev. Dr. Don L. Davis

SECOND EDITION

TUMI Press
3701 East Thirteenth Street North
Wichita, Kansas 67208

Becoming Like Your Teacher:
Developing Effective Church Planting Apprenticeships

First edition 2018, Second edition 2019.

The Urban Ministry Institute
3701 East 13th Street North
Wichita, KS 67208

ISBN: 978-1-62932-324-4

Published by TUMI Press
A division of World Impact, Inc.

The Urban Ministry Institute is a ministry of World Impact, Inc.

Table of Contents

Preface

He also told them a parable: "Can a blind man lead a blind man? Will they not both fall into a pit? A disciple is not above his teacher, but everyone when he is fully trained will be like his teacher."

~ Luke 6.39-40

Leadership is very much following somebody who presumes to know exactly where we need to go.

Jesus provides this simple definition of leadership to explain the necessity of every leader to be worthy of a follower-ship. Isn't it obvious that a person who cannot see, who is actually blind, should not be in the business of leading others around? Following such a person will inevitably not end well – "will they not both fall into a pit?" Jesus teaches that a disciple (a learner dedicated to follow the teaching and example of another) is not above his teacher, but, after the training process is fully complete, it is enough that the disciple "will be like his teacher." Here, Jesus gives a clear definition of discipleship: becoming like your teacher.

Such a simple formula should not be ignored. Training requires a teacher, someone worthy to be followed, someone whose experience, judgment, and understanding place them in a role to train and teach others. It also requires a disciple, someone who willingly and voluntarily submits themselves to the regimen, discipline, and training that a teacher provides. The end of the process is identification: after the disciple is fully trained, he will become just like his teacher. Real discipling, by this definition, is a form of apprenticeship.

An apprentice is a person who works for another to learn a trade or skill, historically, a learner who binds herself to a master craftsman in order to become a master herself. This idea of being bound to another to become like them is a fundamental way of learning all things, shown in the most natural and informal manner to the most skilled professional tradesmen. Perhaps the best way to learn a skill or trade is to find a person who is expert at it, and learn from the association. You watch them, accompany them, learn from them as they supervise you, allow yourself to be taught, corrected, and coached by them in order to become like them. This form of learning is simple, clean, efficient, and effective. All you need is a master and a student able and willing to pay the price to learn from the master.

We are convinced that for church planting, no method is as efficient and effective as apprenticeship. The best way to "apprehend" (to grasp the meaning of, to understand and perceive) a skill is to learn under someone who themselves have apprehended it first. To come under a leader in a field is the best way to learn the field. This is the standard for a number of trades: medicine, science, academics, construction, and music. The best way to understand something in that field is to learn it from someone well schooled, long experienced, and deeply trained in the field. This wisdom can be powerfully embraced in our church planting and pastoring contexts. When a disciple is fully trained, Jesus asserts, they will become just like their teacher.

While this does suggest that a bad teacher will train bad disciples, it also asserts that strong, clear teachers will equip strong clear disciples. At a time when we need scores of young, aggressive, and effective church planters, the call for apprenticeship programs and mentors must go out strong. We need churches, church plants, and outreach ministries to open their doors and their hearts to designing and hosting apprenticeship programs that will multiply the number of effective, emerging leaders as quickly as possible. No other form of leadership development is as clear, compelling, and compassionate as apprenticeships; multiplying the number of worthy interns and candidates to learn the art and skill of church planting could revolutionize our impact in urban mission and outreach, and in the number of souls won to Christ.

This booklet is only meant to be a primer, a "tablespoon out of the pot" tidbit of the good wisdom and insights associated with church planting apprenticeships. If reading this tract makes the reader either more willing to prayerfully consider starting an apprenticeship program, or becoming an apprentice, its creation will be worth the effort. Join us in identifying a generation of worthy church planters who can be apprenticed to learn how to plant and prosper healthy communities of Christ in neighborhoods where he is not yet known and worshiped. Let us invest in an army of candidates ready to reproduce themselves for the sake of the Kingdom. Read this tract carefully. Start right away. The Spirit will lead you, and you will bear fruit, the kind that remains and multiplies.

Bob Engel, Newark, New Jersey
Don Davis, Wichita, Kansas
August 9, 2018

Introduction

War – Hard apprenticeship of Freedom.

~ Edward Everett Hale

With the incarnation and ministry of Jesus of Nazareth, the Messiah, the Kingdom of God has come! Christ Jesus has made a public spectacle of Satan, his minions, and all that the Kingdom of Darkness represents. He is God's Champion and Commander of his heavenly hosts. At the same time the Kingdom is yet to come. We live in the age of the Church who presses forward in the expansion and advancement of the Kingdom of God. As C. S. Lewis stated, "Enemy-occupied territory – that is what this world is. Christianity is the story of how the rightful king has landed, you might say landed in disguise, and is calling us to take part in a great campaign of sabotage."

You are following in the footsteps and calling of the first saboteurs, the Apostle Paul and Barnabas (Acts 11.25, 26, 30; 12.25; 13.1-3). Like them and the countless missionary saints after them, we all must enter into an apprentice phase until that time comes when the Spirit of the Lord, through the Elders, says, "Set apart for me Barnabas and Paul for the work to which I have called them."

Whether you are hosting such a program or believe that God has called you to participate within one, you will need to trust the Lord to provide you with all you will require to fulfill your duty in Christ. We all must gladly submit to that full range of responsibilities as servants in the church for the purpose of being set apart by the Holy Spirit to engage in the Great Commission of our Lord Jesus. As his ambassador, you are called to evangelize, make disciples, raise up leaders and establish a new church in "enemy-occupied territory" for the glory of God.

Being a representative for Jesus with the task of planting an outpost of the Kingdom of God requires nothing less than a ready response to his call to ministry, sharing the life of Christ as his chosen vessel and servant. As the demon told the sons of Sceva, referring to authentic spiritual identity, "Jesus I know, and Paul I recognize" (Acts 19.15b). With the foundation of Christ confirmed in you and the mantle of his calling upon you, you can both offer or undergo rigorous and disciplined church planting training. If you are hosting an apprenticeship program, you can be God's chosen instrument to raise up laborers for Christ. If you are called as an apprentice, you can be equipped in order that you may become competent and fully assured to go and accomplish the task the Lord has given you.

Code of Conduct
TUMI's Mission-Critical Perspectives

When you are deployed in enemy-occupied territory to establish a church (which literally is an outpost of the Kingdom of God), you will encounter spiritual opposition. Our spiritual combatant, the evil one, has gone before you and filled your target area with spiritual land mines and barriers designed to wound, kill, and destroy you and your team. His goal is to sabotage your efforts, rendering inoperative your work and the task you have been called and commissioned to accomplish. Our perspectives regarding our task and end are like metal detectors that give you a warning when you sweep over a potential mine. They are more than sufficient to help you side-step and eliminate these spiritual mines of destruction.

Now is the time, as a church planter apprentice, to know your "metal detector." Church planters and their team are involved in making hundreds of decisions every day. The decisions they make are built upon clearly articulated and held perspectives that shape your actions, and determine your strategies. Indeed, your perspectives help to direct you towards your specific purpose, that particular calling and task that the risen Lord has commissioned you to accomplish. This unique calling has been affirmed and recognized by Christ's Church and confirmed by his own Holy Spirit.

When walking through enemy-occupied territory, you will refer and reflect upon your perspectives in order to:

1. *Make decisions.* We make a deliberate choice to focus on what is important to us. Your perspectives shape your values, which when affirmed and shared, mobilizes your team into a cohesive squad.

2. *Stand strong.* When the enemy attacks your mind with his deceptive lies about who you are in Christ, your biblically informed perspectives will empower you to stand strong. Your worth is built on who God declares you to be in Christ. Who you are is more important than what you do.

3. *Give focus.* When the task becomes too much, unclear, or a formidable struggle, your renewed perspectives provide focus, direction, motivation to not shrink back but to believe and press onward.

TUMI's Mission-Critical Perspectives

The Calling of God

And we know that for those who love God all things work together for good, for those who are called according to his purpose.

~ Romans 8.28

We do all we do fully assured that God is at this very moment calling, gifting, and anointing men and women in the city to represent his interests there, and are convinced that these chosen city leaders will be the vessels through whom he advances his Kingdom.

The Kingdom of God

But seek first the kingdom of God and his righteousness, and all these things will be added to you.

~ Matthew 6.33

We are burdened to see the freedom, wholeness, and justice of the Kingdom of God embodied, celebrated, and proclaimed in church communities who show visibly what the "Rule of God" looks like when it is embraced by people who acknowledge Christ's lordship.

The Centrality of the Church

. . . if I delay, you may know how one ought to behave in the household of God, which is the church of the living God, a pillar and buttress of the truth.

~ 1 Timothy 3.15

We hold deeply the conviction that effective ministry takes place in the Body of Christ, the agent of the Kingdom, where we facilitate the multiplication of healthy, reproducing urban churches, especially among the poor.

The Power of Community

Now you are the body of Christ and individually members of it.

~ 1 Corinthians 12.27

We share a passion to employ innovative distance education programming to create and outfit a network of training centers in urban areas that provide excellent, affordable, and spiritually dynamic ministry education that is sensitive to urban culture.

God's Election of the Humble

Listen, my beloved brothers, has not God chosen those who are poor in the world to be rich in faith and heirs of the kingdom, which he has promised to those who love him?

~ James 2.5

We possess a certitude that God has chosen those who are poor in the eyes of this world to be rich in faith and to inherit the Kingdom which he promised to those who love him (James 2.5).

The Standard of Excellence

So, whether you eat or drink, or whatever you do, do all to the glory of God.

~ 1 Corinthians 10.31

We are held by the consuming belief that all effective, credible leadership development demands the requisite formality and rigor of disciplined excellence, with a flat refusal to be remedial or second-class.

The Explosiveness of Multiplication

. . . and what you have heard from me in the presence of many witnesses entrust to faithful men, who will be able to teach others also.

~ 2 Timothy 2.2

We are zealous to facilitate and empower urban church planting movements that share a common spirituality, express freedom in cultural expression, and strategically combine their resources to reach and transform the cities of America and the world.

Call of Duty
Church Planter Apprenticeship

God has created a system in the church whereby we can equip emerging leaders to accomplish his will under the tutelage of mature mentors and leaders. Apprenticeships are pre-defined terms of service and learning sponsored in the context of a supportive church/ministry, overseen by capable supervision which is designed to equip the apprentice in church planting among the poor.

"Pre-defined terms of service and learning." Apprenticeships should be limited to a specific term of service, with specific rules and guidelines for its length and work. We strongly suggest that you create a written contract of service that spells out precisely the bounds, privileges, and responsibilities of the apprenticeship, including its length, any remuneration offered, terms of service, and all other matters related to the apprentice's work and duties.

". . . in the context of a supportive church/ministry." Apprenticeships should be connected to a particular church or ministry which has formally agreed to oversee the apprentice, providing specific training and exposure to church planting among the poor.

". . . overseen by capable supervision." Apprenticeship's should be connected to specific mentors, supervisors, or leaders who supervise and oversee the apprentice's training, assignments and work. Apprentices should report to these supervisors who equip, encourage, and offer regular feedback as to the apprentice's progress or areas of growth needed to be worked on.

". . . which is designed to equip the apprentice in church planting among the poor." Apprenticeships are targeted to equip the individual to plant a church among the poor. Apprenticeships are not "special" in the sense of creating some unique and unrelated role for the apprentice. Rather, the best apprenticeship programs are connected specifically to training the apprentice to gain expertise and exposure for the task of planting a church that the church/ministry currently embraces, supports, and enhances the goals and priorities of that church/ministry.

Training interns in a wisely-supervised apprenticeship program is an effective means to multiply spiritual laborers for the harvest, and to equip servant-leaders for effective ministry in the church!

The Battle Plan
Confirm and Equip

From the start, we should assume that ministry candidates will come to us at various levels of maturity and development, i.e., in their overall understanding of Scripture, living a Christ-centered life and missions. Each indigenous urban church planter must already possess the requisite maturity and experience to be considered a worthy candidate in an apprenticeship program.

Indeed, a solid apprenticeship requires great care and focus done well in advance of the learning experience to guarantee its success. In other words, ministry supervisors must take the time to map out a measurable and feasible apprentice plan and overall schedule. In addition, time must be given to determine the substance of the apprenticeship, including assignments, field work, time for study and critical reflection, and whatever financial resources and staff support the apprenticeship program will provide. Until these critical features have been carefully considered and decided, no church plant apprenticeship program should be commenced!

It is foundational that any individual who wants to enlist into an Apprentice Program, must have the blessing and confirmation of his/her leaders. It is the church leadership who must discern and confirm the individuals calling and gifting. Great care and focus must be decided well in advance of the apprenticeship to guarantee its success. The Apostle Paul, though called and gifted by the Lord Jesus himself, still submitted himself to the leadership of the local church in Antioch.

The leadership of a local church has the final say-so for those seeking confirmation to serve in a church planter apprenticeship program. Online programs, written tests, or the individual's "feelings" are all subservient to the leadership in which the prospective apprentice submits and honors. Outside aids can be a supplement for leadership as they pray and seek the Spirit's leading and confirmation. One such aid is TUMI's* Evangel Church Planter's Assessment. This excellent tool can assist church leadership in their vetting process.

There are four areas of church planter training that are foundational to Designing your Church Planter Apprenticeship Program. These are:

1. *Leadership Development.* "Survival of the fittest is not the same as survival of the best. Leaving leadership development up to chance is foolish" (Morgan McCall). Designing your leadership development track requires prayer and intentionality. One size does not fit all. Leaders are made, not born. You must know your apprentice and what they need to make them into a leader.

---

* The Urban Ministry Institute (TUMI), the national training arm for World Impact, equips leadership for the urban church, especially among the poor, in order to advance the Kingdom of God. We focus our investment on those called to evangelize, disciple, plant, and pastor churches in unreached urban neighborhoods. Our single passion and desire is to identify, empower, and release laborers who can both display and declare God's kingdom reign among their neighbors, where they live. Learn more by going to: *www.tumi.org.*

For example, Dr. Davis's (Executive Director, The Urban
Ministry Institute) *Get Your Pretense On!* outlines a biblical
and doctrinal perspective designed to help any disciple of
Christ know what it means to act worthy of your true, redeemed
status and position, and to make a difference in the roles
where Jesus has placed you. Two of the chapters, "There's
Plenty Good Room: The Centrality of the Church in God's
Kingdom Advance", and "The *Oikos* Factor: Being Used of
God to Change Your World" are excellent readings for dialogue
and discussion in your church planter apprentice regimen.
The concepts in this book will prove invaluable for your
apprentice in their leadership development.

2. *Biblical and Theological Training.* *"As we have said before, so
    now I say again: If anyone is preaching to you a gospel contrary
    to the one you received, let him be accursed"* (Gal. 1.9).

    From the beginning of history, the enemy has sought to twist
    and malign God's Word. A half-truth is always a full lie. The
    Church's history is filled with women and men who sacrificed
    their lives for the defense of the Church's confession, what
    it has "believed everywhere, always and by all." A solid
    apprenticeship program respects this; a good one always
    has a quality biblical and theological training component.

    Thousands of students and hundreds of satellites use The
    Urban Ministry Institute's *Capstone Curriculum* around the
    world. This resource, as well as hundreds of other curriculum
    resources, are available to you as you design your own, unique
    and personalized apprenticeship program to hone in on your
    apprentice's biblical and theological areas of growth.

3. *Church Planting Experience* (Field Work/Boots on the Ground). *"And he appointed twelve (whom he also named apostles) so that they might be with him and he might send them out to preach"* (Mark 3.14).

   An apprenticeship is not just about books to read and assignments to be completed. The best apprenticeships occur when the pastor and other leaders personally invest into the life of the apprentice. Jesus prayed and called twelve apostles to *"be with him."* He spent time with them, asked them questions, invited them to participate with him in ministry, and eventually sent them out to make disciples of all nations. In effective discipleship, there is simply no substitute for individualized, personal, and relational investment.

4. *Spiritual Growth.* "Therefore let us leave the elementary doctrine of Christ and go on to maturity, not laying again a foundation of repentance from dead works and of faith toward God" (Heb. 6.1).

   God expects each of his children to mature in Christ, to develop into full adults in him. Like our own children, such maturity will not happen overnight nor by chance. Good loving parental care is intentional. Such care provides input for the purpose of maturity, and it necessarily implements the refining responsibilities along each of life's growth stages. Just like a developing child, in similar fashion, an apprentice needs the necessary spiritual formation to grow into a mature disciple. That maturity is essential for each one who feels called to serve the Commander of the Lords Army in every situation.

One of the great problems in our contemporary spiritual formation is the sheer number of diverse, non-integrated ideas, resources, and themes in the ongoing lives of Christian communities today. This patchwork of disconnected approaches and ideas rubs against our natural disposition to focus on an idea, one big, integrated idea for an extended period. For those of us who see Christ Jesus as the source and center of the Christian experience, this recurring focus on dozens of disconnected ideas sabotages effective, biblical spiritual formation.

It is our conviction that God can deepen us in a single spiritual concept for an entire year, with focused disciplined study and reflection for most of it. The Urban Ministry Institute's *Sacred Roots Annual* centers the apprentice's life around a shared theme for the entire journey of the Church Year. The apprentice can effectively then become focused on a single spiritual theme for the entire year rather than being scattered around a multitude of themes. Such a focus can enable your church family and community to center itself on a Christ-centered focus, one that allows you to grow deeper around a significant biblical theme that the Spirit wishes you to know, feel, and experience together.

These are just a few examples of the many tools that are available to you from the TUMI church planting arsenal. You design your apprenticeship program to fit your vision and goals. TUMI deliberately seeks to strengthen your hand as you design and run your own program, for the purposes and ends that you have set for it. From a spiritual perspective, TUMI adopts the old Home Depot slogan, "You can do it! We can help."

Field Ready
Six Fitness Marks
before Commissioning

The Armed Services Vocational Aptitude Battery (ASVAB) is a multiple-choice test, administered by the United States Military Entrance Processing Command, used to determine qualification for enlistment in the United States Armed Forces. To enter into the Special Forces, individuals have to reach the highest marks on the ASVAB tests. If these predetermined marks are not attained, the individual doesn't move into the Special Forces. They move into a different roll within the Military.

Scriptures mandate and give examples to, "not be too quick on the laying of hands." If not taken seriously, great harm can come upon the individual and the Community. We are in a spiritual war and the enemy is out to kill, steal, and destroy. Everyone is called to engage and participate in God's kingdom movement but not everyone has the same calling. The calling to evangelize, make disciples and establish a new church is not a calling for everyone.

Before commissioning individuals to church plant, there are six marks that must clearly be a part of the church planter. A quality apprenticeship program will strengthen each of these marks so that in partnership with the Holy Spirit, leadership can say, "Now set apart for me." These marks are:

1. *Master the art and discipline of being a worthy leader.* The apprentice must be able to feed themselves spiritually through a variety of spiritual disciplines (1 Tim. 4.7-8). The task of church planting requires, demands, one who is sensitive to the leading of the Holy Spirit and is quick to respond in obedience (Acts 16.6-10).

2. *Engage in personal evangelism and spiritual warfare.* The apprentice must know how to engage in evangelism that leads the hearer to a point of response. Engaging spiritual warfare through prayer will be foundational (Rom. 1.16; Eph. 6.18).

3. *Follow up new Christians and disciple them in the spiritual disciplines.* The apprentice must know how to lead a convert to be a disciple of Jesus. He/she has to be skilled in doing this through formal curriculum and life relationships (Matt. 28.19-20).

4. *Do the work of a pastor, shepherding others and fulfilling pastoral responsibilities.* The apprentice must have the necessary gifts, character, and skills to "shepherd the flock."

5. *Understand and be committed to the principles of spiritual reproduction and church planting movements.* There must be clear observation and communication from the Apprentice that, "none should perish." The apprentice must understand the vastness of the harvest field and the importance of reproduction and multiplying themselves to create church planting movements (2 Tim. 2.2; 1 Thess. 1.8).

6. *Possess a strategic vision for contributing to the Great Commission, and a practical plan to implement it.* The apprentice must have a vision from the Lord that burns within them and a plan to unleash this Spirit given vision. To assist in helping birth the vision through a Spirit driven strategic process we recommend enlisting into the *Evangel School of Urban Church Planting.* (Visit *www.tumi.org* for more details.)

Checklist
All Systems Are Go!

We are held by the consuming belief that all effective, credible leadership development demands the requisite formality and rigor of disciplined excellence, with a flat refusal to be remedial or second-class. To ensure that quality is maintained, your program should commit to cover all the major areas of both designing and managing an effective apprenticeship program. All elements of the program must be done excellently, in proper order, and professionally carried out for the benefit of both the church and the apprentice. This following checklist will assist you in developing an excellent apprentice program for the glory of God and the furtherance of his Kingdom.

YOUR APPRENTICESHIP PROGRAM CHECKLIST

Determine the Area Your Apprenticeships Will Be Offered (Choose all that apply)

❑ Church Planter

❑ Pastoral Care

❑ Worship/Music

❑ Children and Youth Ministry

❑ Teacher

❑ Counselor

Sketch the General Shape and Scope of Your Proposed Apprenticeship

❑ Think through the details of your Battle Plan (See pages 19-23).

❑ Define precisely the purpose of this apprenticeship. *State concisely why you are hosting it.*

❑ What ministry areas will be impacted by this apprenticeship? *Where will it occur?*

❑ Qualifications (age, education, character). *What demands do you need for candidates to meet?*

❑ When/Duration. *How long do you envision the apprenticeship to last?*

❑ Time Commitment. *How much time will you allot to the apprenticeship investment per week?*

❑ Remuneration. *How much money/support do you intend to provide to the apprentice?*

❑ Housing. *If housing is a portion of your support, where will it be, and what will it involve?*

Create and Circulate Your Candidate Application Form

❑ Contact Information. *Obtain all personal contact information needed for the candidate including name, address, phone, e-mail, etc.*

❑ Testimony (paragraph). *Have the candidate list their personal story of their journey to Jesus, their personal walk and faith, and their ongoing life in Christ today.*

❑ Goals of the Apprenticeship. *The candidate should list their goals and objectives (their expectations) for the apprenticeship.*

❑ Legal record (if any). *Have the candidate list any history they may have had with law enforcement, any pending situations, or any convictions as it relates to the law and the state.*

❑ Doctrinal Response Questions. *Have the candidate respond to your statement of faith, listing their commitment to represent it, and willingness to abide by its strictures.*

❑ Statement of Faith Agreement. *Have the candidate sign your statement of faith.*

❑ Recommendation. *Ensure lead pastor and relevant staff accept the candidate's choice.*

Map Out Carefully How You Will Deal with Issues and Rough Edges (Rules of Engagement)

❑ Think through scenarios and map out how you will deal with tough situations (*e.g., insubordination, ineffective work, moral compromise, conflict management*).

❑ Detail the accountability structure you will have for the apprenticeship (*e.g., weekly review meetings covering both spiritual growth and ministerial responsibility*).

❑ Communicate clearly the supervisory structure (*e.g., what are they responsible for, to who will they report, how often, what form [whether face-to-face, written, both?]*).

❑ Provide instruction in how to handle emergency situations during the apprenticeship (*e.g., who to contact, things to be aware of, procedures for at-risk circumstances*).

Finalize and Implement Your Internship/Apprenticeship Program

❑ Formally interview, consider, and offer the apprenticeship opportunity to your selected candidate.

❑ Announce your selection to the staff and congregation.

❑ Prepare for the apprenticeship's launch date, and arrange all necessary details to implement it.

❑ Implement the Apprenticeship program, adapting your schedule and content as you go.

❑ Once completed, recognize the intern, formally celebrating their accomplishment and contribution.

❑ Counsel the apprentice on what the next steps should be not that the apprenticeship has been completed.

Let's Take This City for God

From the time of Pentecost, the apostolic-missionary movement has unfurled through the centuries to herald the Good News of redemption to the lost. That Good News is clear: when unbelievers respond to the Gospel in believing faith and confession, they are free from the penalty of sin, transferred into Christ's Kingdom of righteousness, joy and peace. Since the time of the apostles, God has looked for select men and women who are filled with his Spirit to courageously go and make disciples of all the nations. Today, the "nations" (people groups) of the world have migrated to our inner cities. Quite literally, if we take our cities for God through the proclamation of the Gospel and making disciples of the faithful, we can reach the nations of the world and not even cross an ocean! The peoples of the world have come to our doorstep; all we need is the resolve to win them, gather them into outposts of the Kingdom, and see them deployed to their kin folk and neighbors as ambassadors of Jesus Christ.

Let us always be aware that in this expansion of God's kingdom authority in the earth we face a ruthless and cunning enemy, who is determined to undermine all that we do as we seek to obey our Lord. Of course, the Church Militant has been given her mission orders from her Lord. Our King Jesus, triumphant and risen, is undeterred by the enemy's opposition. Even in the face of what appears to be insurmountable odds, he has given this specific charge to his church:

> God authorized and commanded me to commission you: Go out and train everyone you meet, far and near, in this way of life, marking them by baptism in the threefold name: Father, Son, and Holy Spirit. Then instruct them in the practice of all I have commanded you. I'll be with you as you do this, day after day after day, right up to the end of the age.
>
> ~ Matthew 28.19-20, *The Message*

In light of our Lord's command, then, this is the time to experiment, to be courageous. J. Oswald Sanders has said, "A great deal more failure is the result of an excess of caution than of bold experimentation with new ideas. The frontiers of the Kingdom of God were never advanced by men and women of caution." Too much is at stake for us to be "men and women of caution." We need more church planters, more folk called by God with apostolic gifting willing to go and make disciples of Jesus among the lost. How do we obtain them? We apprentice a new generation, ready and willing to respond!

We should remember always that the concept of apprenticeship is not a new idea. It continues to undergird the preparation of excellence in a number of fields (e.g., medicine, construction, academics), although it often times seems ignored or absent in our churches. The Evangel movement calls on the urban church to make alive this ancient way of raising up leaders once again.

Above all other things, we must embrace the Lord's command afresh. Let us not be the first Church era that fails and falters in our obedience to the commission of the Captain of the Lord's Army. Rather, may we together become that generation of Christ followers who surrender everything to take our cities for God. Let us give our all to equip thousands upon thousands of apprentices whom the Spirit will deploy as some of the finest, most dedicated cadres of church planters that the modern missionary venture has ever witnessed. And, our heartfelt prayer is this: let this miracle happen among the poorest of the poor, the least of these, in the toughest, most unreached communities on the earth.

"So let it be written! So let it be done!"

The Nicene Creed with Biblical Support

We believe in one God,
  (Deut. 6.4-5; Mark 12.29; 1 Cor. 8.6)
the Father Almighty,
  (Gen. 17.1; Dan. 4.35; Matt. 6.9; Eph. 4.6; Rev. 1.8)
Maker of heaven and earth
  (Gen. 1.1; Isa. 40.28; Rev. 10.6)
and of all things visible and invisible.
  (Ps. 148; Rom. 11.36; Rev. 4.11)

We believe in one Lord Jesus Christ, the only Begotten Son of
  God, begotten of the Father before all ages, God from God,
  Light from Light, True God from True God, begotten not
  created, of the same essence as the Father,
  (John 1.1-2; 3.18; 8.58; 14.9-10; 20.28; Col. 1.15, 17; Heb. 1.3-6)
through whom all things were made.
  (John 1.3; Col. 1.16)

Who for us men and for our salvation came down from heaven
   and was incarnate by the Holy Spirit and the Virgin Mary and
   became human.
   (Matt. 1.20-23; John 1.14; 6.38; Luke 19.10)
Who for us too, was crucified under Pontius Pilate, suffered
   and was buried.
   *(Matt. 27.1-2; Mark 15.24-39, 43-47; Acts 13.29; Rom. 5.8;
   Heb. 2.10; 13.12)*
The third day he rose again according to the Scriptures,
   (Mark 16.5-7; Luke 24.6-8; Acts 1.3; Rom. 6.9; 10.9; 2 Tim. 2.8)
ascended into heaven, and is seated at the right hand of the
   Father.
   (Mark 16.19; Eph. 1.19-20)
He will come again in glory to judge the living and the dead,
   and his Kingdom will have no end.
   *(Isa. 9.7; Matt. 24.30; John 5.22; Acts 1.11; 17.31; Rom. 14.9;
   2 Cor. 5.10; 2 Tim. 4.1)*

We believe in the Holy Spirit, the Lord and life-giver,
   *(Gen. 1.1-2; Job 33.4; Ps. 104.30; 139.7-8; Luke 4.18-19;
   John 3.5-6; Acts 1.1-2; 1 Cor. 2.11; Rev. 3.22)*
who proceeds from the Father and the Son,
   (John 14.16-18, 26; 15.26; 20.22)
who together with the Father and Son is worshiped and glorified,
   (Isa. 6.3; Matt. 28.19; 2 Cor. 13.14; Rev. 4.8)
who spoke by the prophets.
   (Num. 11.29; Mic. 3.8; Acts 2.17-18; 2 Pet. 1.21)

We believe in one holy, catholic, and apostolic Church.
   *(Matt. 16.18; Eph. 5.25-28; 1 Cor. 1.2; 10.17; 1 Tim. 3.15;
   Rev. 7.9)*

We acknowledge one baptism for the forgiveness of sin,
(Acts 22.16; 1 Pet. 3.21; Eph. 4.4-5)
And we look for the resurrection of the dead and the life of
the age to come.
(Isa. 11.6-10; Mic. 4.1-7; Luke 18.29-30; Rev. 21.1-5; 21.22-22.5)
Amen.

The Nicene Creed with Biblical Support – Memory Verses

Below are suggested memory verses, one for each section of
the Creed.

The Father
Rev. 4.11 – Worthy are you, our Lord and God, to receive glory
and honor and power, for you created all things, and by your
will they existed and were created.

The Son
John 1.1 – In the beginning was the Word, and the Word was
with God, and the Word was God.

The Son's Mission
1 Cor. 15.3-5 – For what I received I passed on to you as of
first importance: that Christ died for our sins according to the
Scriptures, that he was buried, that he was raised on the third
day according to the Scriptures, and that he appeared to Peter,
and then to the Twelve.

The Holy Spirit
Rom. 8.11 – If the Spirit of him who raised Jesus from the dead dwells in you, he who raised Christ Jesus from the dead will also give life to your mortal bodies through his Spirit who dwells in you.

The Church
1 Pet. 2.9 – But you are a chosen race, a royal priesthood, a holy nation, a people for his own possession, that you may proclaim the excellencies of him who called you out of darkness into his marvelous light.

Our Hope
1 Thess. 4.16-17 – For the Lord himself will descend from heaven with a cry of command, with the voice of an archangel, and with the sound of the trumpet of God. And the dead in Christ will rise first. Then we who are alive, who are left, will be caught up together with them in the clouds to meet the Lord in the air, and so we will always be with the Lord.

Steps to Equipping Others

Rev. Dr. Don L. Davis

Step One

You become a Master at it, striving toward mastery by practicing it with regularity, excellence, and enjoyment. You must learn to do it, and do it excellently. While you need not be perfect, you should be able to do it, be doing it regularly, and growing in your practice of it. This is the most fundamental principle of all mentoring and discipling. You cannot teach what you do not know or cannot do, and when your Apprentice is fully trained, they will become like you (Luke 6.40).

Step Two

You select an Apprentice who also desires to develop mastery of the thing, one who is teachable, faithful, and available. Jesus called the Twelve to be with him, and to send them out to preach (Mark 3.14). His relationship was clear, neither vague nor coerced. The roles and responsibilities of the relationship must be carefully outlined, clearly discussed, and openly agreed upon.

Step Three

You instruct and model the task in the presence of and accompanied by your Apprentice. He/she comes alongside you to listen, observe, and watch. You do it with regularity and excellence, and your

Apprentice comes along "for the ride," who is brought along to see how it is done. A picture is worth a thousand words. This sort of non-pressure participant observation is critical to in-depth training (2 Tim. 2.2; Phil. 4.9).

Step Four

You do the task and practice the thing together. Having modeled the act for your Apprentice in many ways and at many times, you now invite them to cooperate with you by becoming a partner-in-training, working together on the task. The goal is to do the task together, taking mutual responsibility. You coordinate your efforts, working together in harmony to accomplish the thing.

Step Five

Your Apprentice does the task on their own, in the presence of and accompanied by you. You provide opportunity to your Apprentice to practice the thing in your presence while you watch and listen. You make yourself available to help, but offer it in the background; you provide counsel, input, and guidance as they request it, but they do the task. Afterwards, you evaluate and clarify anything you may have observed as you accompanied your Apprentice (2 Cor. 11.1).

Step Six

Your Apprentice does the thing solo, practicing it regularly, automatically, and excellently until mastery of the thing is gained. After your Apprentice has done the task under your supervision excellently, he/she is ready to be released to make the thing his/her own by habituating the act in his/her own life. You are a co-doer with your Apprentice; both of you are doing the task without coercion or aid from the other. The goal is familiarity and skillfulness in the task (Heb. 5.11-15).

Step Seven

*Your Apprentice **becomes a Mentor of others**, selecting other faithful Apprentices to equip and train.* The training process bears fruit when the Apprentice, having mastered the thing you have equipped him/her to do, becomes a trainer of others. This is the heart of the discipling and training process (Heb. 5.11-14; 2 Tim. 2.2).

From Seeker to Sensei: Developing Effective Movement Apprenticeships

Rev. Dr. Don L. Davis

A disciple is not above his teacher, but everyone when he is fully trained will be like his teacher.

~ Jesus, Luke 6.40 (ESV)

Seeker: a person or thing that seeks

~ dictionary.com
https://www.dictionary.com/browse/seeker?s=t

Sensei: (can be pronounced "Sensai" as well), Sinsang, Sonsaeng, Seonsaeng or Xiansheng is an honorific term shared in Chinese honorifics and Japanese honorifics that is translated as "person born before another" or "one who comes before."

~ Wikipedia
https://en.wikipedia.org/wiki/Sensei

I. The *Paradigm* of Apprenticeships: Movements, Leaders, and Apprenticeships

A. The Golden Strand: How do movements start, grow, and thrive?

1. *Strand one:* The role of the founder: Moses

2. *Strand two:* The synergy of the "first followers": Joshua

3. *Strand three:* The strength of young apprentices in a tradition: Jehu, Gideon, Samson, Samuel

4. The power of tradition: not a dirty word

   a. *paradosis:* the handing down to another the invaluable deposit

   b. A mixture of content and loyalty

   c. *Traditioned innovation* (Dr. Alvin Sanders): building on the legacy given, engaging on the situation encountered

B. Why apprenticeships work among movements among the poor

   1. They are *organic:* receiving protection, care, and training from another.

   2. They are *affordable:* they require presence not funds.

   3. They are *transparent:* you learn on the job in the presence of a valid leader.

   4. They are *reliable:* authority is given after verified loyalty and service.

5. They are *reproducible*: once a system of apprenticeship is begun, it can be replicated indefinitely.

C. The biblical blueprint of a worthy apprenticeship

1. The call of *God*: a publicly acknowledged and confirmed call

2. The character of *Christ*: proven character in the midst of lived life

3. The charisma of the *Holy Spirit*: anointing and gifting in the Church

4. The connection to the *Church community*: compelling testimony within and among the people of the body

II. The *Process* of Apprenticeships: From Seeker to Sensei (*Steps to Equipping Others*)

A. Join the movement and commit to represent its identity, purpose, and mission.

B. Distinguish yourself in the movement as a champion of faithfulness of service.

C. Receive apprentices for future representation and authority in the movement.

D. Instruct and model movement representation task in the presence of and accompanied by the apprentices.

E. Co-labor in movement representation as colleagues and comrades together.

F. Give the apprentice solo assignments, with you only accompanying as support.

G. Assign the apprentice formal leadership status, i.e., to take on their own apprenticeships as agent of the movement.

III. **The *Principle* of Apprenticeship: Leadership as Representation (*The Role of Fomal Proxy: Leadership as Representation*)**

A. Apostles, evangelists, prophets, and ambassadors: representatives of another

B. Jesus as the perfect pattern of the representative of God

C. The dynamics of representation

1. The *Commissioning*: formal selection and call

2. The *Equipping*: appropriate training and investment

3. The *Entrustment*: endowed with the authority and power to act on behalf of the movement

4. The *Mission*: faithful execution of the task

5. The *Reckoning*: assessment and evaluation of the results attained

6. The *Reward*: recognition and reward based on the faithful service and results attained

IV. The *Problems* of Apprenticeships: The Rough Edges of Apprenticeship

A. *Movement creep*: Unclear as to what the movement is, stands for, or seeks to do

B. *Secret society*: No discernible path to join or align with our movement

C. *Unspoken pathways*: Neglect of specific ways movement folk can engage and represent the movement, whatever the level

D. *Phony channels of opportunity*: tolerating unhealthy folk or promoting folk with unproven track records among us

E. *No recognition or promotion*: failing to reward loyalty and service

V. The *Practice* of Apprenticeships: Take-aways for a New Vision

A. Clarify your movement play-book: Who, what, why, how . . .

B. Make the invitation: boldly, clearly, and often.

C. Ask God for insight into your choice of the next generation of leaders.

D. Offer specific roles, assignments for the most loyal "first followers."

E. Develop a workable, modest apprenticeship program, focused on investment.

F. Provide both oversight, provision, and answerability throughout the entire period.

G. Certify your apprentices: be ready to delegate the assignments and authority once the program is successfully completed.

Closing quotes from Sensei Mr. Miyagi

"Either you karate do 'yes' or karate do 'no.' You karate do 'guess so,' (get squished) just like grape."

The point: Once you commit to an enterprise, do it with your full heart and effort. Or not, and pay the price.

"Never trust a spiritual leader who cannot dance."

The point: Every true leader has to be flexible, adaptable, and able to enjoy themselves in the process. Correction and celebration!

Made in the USA
Columbia, SC
13 February 2025

53741928R00028